FROM O
RUSTIC GARD

A miscellany of topical, humorous and nostalgic verse

Patricia Anne Booth

ARTHUR H. STOCKWELL LTD.
Elms Court Ilfracombe
Devon

First published in Great Britain, 1990

ISBN 0 7223 2476-6
Printed in Great Britain by
Arthur H. Stockwell Ltd.
Elms Court Ilfracombe
Devon

CONTENTS

OUR RUSTIC GARDEN SEAT

In the centre of our lawn,
  Standing there with pride,
A handsome rustic seat,
  Sturdy, strong and wide.

It waits with quiet patience,
  This garden centre-piece,
We treat it with affection,
  For its uses never cease.

Among its many virtues,
  A support for saw and hammer,
Leaning post for bicycles,
  And prop for steps and ladder.

A scratching post for pussies,
  To sharpen up their claws,
Or perch on after breakfast,
  When washing fur and paws.

On sunny days in Summer,
  We relax the easiest,
With feet resting upon it,
  To take a well-earned rest.

Clothed in Winter's snow,
  The icicles will cling,
But our seat is not forgotten,
  As it awaits the coming Spring.

Late on misty evenings,
  When slowly fades the light,
We peep outside the window,
  To see a moving sight.

There within the garden,
  Very real and near,
Ghosts of people past,
  In person do appear.

Our seat can hold the images,
And show them when it may,
Of folk who loved our garden,
As we do today.

So when we leave for Heaven,
And pack our memories neat,
High on the list will surely be,
Our Rustic Garden Seat.

GREEN CHEESE

I'm sure you've seen me quite often,
On my face is a permanent smile,
And not being very adventurous,
You'll notice I'm here all the while.

I live entirely alone,
Where no-one passes my way,
So I'm yearning for somebody's company,
To help enliven my day.

I keep my home reasonably tidy,
And try not to skip any chore,
But with ground exceptionally dusty,
Gardening is rather a bore.

I can't take a holiday outing,
Or sun myself on a warm beach,
A day trip is out of the question,
For alas, there's no sea within reach

All that I eat is green cheese,
This place is full of the stuff,
But of such a monotonous diet,
I'm thinking enough is enough.

And I don't see my neighbours at all,
They're rather a long way from me,
Nonetheless there's a permanent 'invite',
For them to call round for tea.

So, you're welcome to visit anon,
Though my comforts are simple and few,
Just ample fresh air and solitude,
At my home with a wonderful view.

And I hope those adventurous spacemen,
Will be landing here again soon,
Because it's rather a lonely existence,
Being the *Man On The Moon*.

CHINA PAINTING

When the time arrived,
   For my annual holiday,
I decided that a hobby,
   Might pass the time away.

An advert caught my eye,
   Which said 'The chance is waiting,
For anyone who's keen,
   To come to China Painting'.

So I packed up my belongings,
   In suitcase and holdall,
Then headed for the rendezvous,
   In a village hall.

But the other folk's equipment,
   Left me at a loss,
They had tiny pots of paint,
   Compared with my large tins of gloss.

On enquiring of the transport,
   For the expedition,
They replied "This is the place,
   We'll receive all our tuition".

They settled round some tables,
 In their chosen spots,
Then brought out an assortment.
 Of vases, plates and pots.

When the class was ready,
 At a given sign,
They embellished each ceramic,
 With a delicate design.

It was then I saw my error,
 And was overcome with gloom,
As my vacation, it appeared,
 Would be spent inside this room.

There would be no trip abroad,
 Which I'd hoped we all might take,
So to the puzzled group,
 I admitted my mistake.

For I'd understood the advert,
 Which offered 'CHINA PAINTING',
Meant we'd all be off to China —
 To do some decorating!

AN ENIGMATIC FELLOW

I've had a special visitor,
  Unique to me, it seems,
No stranger 'being' have I met,
  Even in my dreams.

Of Lilliputian stature,
  With hair a golden sheen,
He wore a one-piece suit,
  In a dazzling shade of green.

I can't decide for certain,
  Though constantly I try,
If he could see me clearly,
  As he only had one eye.

And his voice was somewhat quiet,
  From what I can recall,
In fact, upon reflection,
  He didn't speak at all.

I offered him refreshments,
  For a welcome treat,
But my provisions were rejected,
  As he didn't often eat.

He was an enigmatic fellow,
  Complete with toothless smile,
Yet secretly I hoped,
  He'd linger for a while.

But the time for his departure,
  Inevitably came,
And in my heart I knew,
  We would not meet again.

If anybody feels,
  My tale's beyond belief,
He left behind some proof,
  Of our meeting brief.

For, etched into my lawn,
  Strange markings lie this day,
Circumstantial evidence,
  That he had passed my way.

So he must have been an alien,
  From Jupiter or Mars,
Because he climbed aboard a Spaceship —
  And took off for the Stars.

NEW YEAR RESOLUTION

In keeping with a fairly long tradition,
As each New Year did start,
I'd keenly play my part,
And make myself a New Year Resolution.

I resolved to walk the puppy quite a lot,
At least four times a day,
But my timing went astray,
And the poor pup's now reduced to 'round the block'.

I'd clean the house most thoroughly each week,
Alas I'm months behind,
My duster I can't find,
And now the fluff's a good nine inches deep.

The garden would be weeded, lawn well mown,
Then Spring and Summer passed,
Autumn came at last,
Yet still the grass and weeds surround my home.

Early every morning I'd rise up with the lark,
But this novelty grew thin,
When the nights were drawing in,
For I don't enjoy my breakfast in the dark.

I wouldn't purchase clothes, unless needed without doubt,
Yet again I have spent plenty,
As my purse is rather empty,
Because I *must* just have the latest fashions out.

So I humbly now concede, failure is in sight,
I'm really not too keen,
To follow a régime,
When nothing that I do is ever right.

Therefore my unconventional Resolution,
For the coming year,
Really is quite clear —
To GIVE UP making NEW YEAR RESOLUTIONS!

A HUNDRED POEMS

Is it really me who wrote,
  A full one hundred times,
All these interminable poems,
  With uninspiring rhymes?

This mystery person 'P.A.B.'
  They sound like my initials,
So dare I reasonably assume,
  That folk *read* my epistles?

Perhaps it's all a waste of time,
  Not to mention pencils,
Plus reams of paper gone to waste,
  And other good utensils.

A quick decision I must make,
  In final desperation,
Do I a second hundred write,
  And face more protestations?

Or perhaps it might be easier,
  To earn my 'bread and jam',
If, in the future no-one knows,
  Just who I really am.

So, to disguise my tracks, here is,
  An answer 'Manifico',
I'll change my name, and from now on,
  Be known as 'INCOGNITO!'

I'VE SEEN A BUTTERFLY

"Oh yes, I've seen a butterfly,"
The young child said to me,
"And feathered birds all perched,
On the branches of a tree."

"Such variety of flowers,
Give me great delight,
And all those lofty trees,
Make a wondrous sight."

"I've tasted many fruits,
Plums and bright red cherries,
Pineapples and melons,
Plus juicy sweet blackberries."

* * *

I asked her if the butterflies,
Fly from flower to flower,
Is she content, as I am,
To watch them hour by hour?

And does she hear the birds,
As in the skies they sing,
Whilst on the trees below them,
Leaves rustle in the wind?

Is there a cheerful garden,
Where she can play each dawn,
Midst rose and lilac bushes,
On carefully tended lawn?

Are there ripening fruits,
In an orchard, on display,
Does she pick the flowers,
To make a fine 'nosegay'?

* * *

Yet, as we quietly paused,
  For a moment's grace,
A look of disbelief,
  Spread across her face.

* * *

"But butterflies are fastened,
  With pins onto a board,
How can they possibly fly?
  That is too absurd."

"I cannot pick the flowers,"
  Said she with puzzled look,
"They're only painted pictures,
  In the pages of a book."

"Birds don't float around,
  They're never going places,
Whilst tied onto the trees,
  Contained in large glass cases."

"The earth is made of concrete,
  You can't dig that with ease,
And those who have a garden,
  Must put up plastic trees."

"I've never seen an orchard,
  Or produce from therein,
The only fruits I know,
  Come labelled in a tin."

* * *

With these prophetic answers,
I see within her eyes,
A hundred years of sadness,
At the good Earth's slow demise.

And though I hear her clearly,
'Tis just imagination,
As this child is not yet born,
But from a coming generation.

She's here to warn us all,
If we don't correct it soon,
The way we treat our planet,
Will lead it to its doom.

If we continue as we do,
To destroy with our own hands,
We'll lose all plants and animals,
From right across the lands.

Then she'll never have the pleasure,
Of seeing creatures climb and run,
The only countryside she'll know,
Will be preserved in a museum.

Of nature and its beauty,
There'll be nothing left to see,
For this bewildered youngster,
From the twenty-first century.

AN INSEPARABLE TEAM

You'll see us trotting gaily past forest, field and stream,
All pals side by side,
Matching stride for stride,
An inseparable team.

Our summers are spent grazing atop the mountains high,
Where eagles soar so free,
And larks sing endlessly,
Beneath a clear blue sky.

But tranquil days are over, when Autumn leaves turn gold,
In a stable far away,
We've tasty meadow hay,
And shelter from the cold.

The Winter winds may give one a luminescent nose,
Yet through the drifting snow,
We willingly will go,
For our coats are warm and close.

And reluctant that we are, to leave our comfy bed,
Now the dusk is falling,
We hear our Master calling,
In his cloak of white and red.

"Into your harness Rudolph, it's time to take our leave,
We've many miles to cover,
With presents to deliver,
On this happy Christmas Eve."

WHEN THE CIRCUS CAME TO TOWN

What fun we had those summers,
When the Circus came to Town,
With Harlequins and Tumblers,
And comic red-nosed Clown.

First came the Grand Parade,
Led by a Marching Band,
Whilst coloured spotlights shone,
To create a Wonderland.

In Scarlet Coat and Top Hat,
The Ring-Master was dressed,
Elephants and Camels,
Performed at his request.

Lions jumped through hoops,
With many a snarl and roar,
Some ambidextrous Jugglers,
Made us gasp with awe.

Sea Lions balanced footballs,
With considerable ease,
Above us daring Acrobats,
Swung on a high trapeze.

Lightly on their hind legs,
Chestnut Horses danced,
Then trotted gaily round,
As we gazed entranced.

* * *

But the era of the Circus,
  Was facing its countdown,
And the fateful year arrived,
  When it never came to Town.

So what of those great artistes,
  Animals and all,
When their talents were unwanted,
  What fate did they befall?

The brightly plaited Horses,
  Who always stole the scene,
Were finally unsaddled,
  And retired to pastures green.

Upon a distant wasteland,
  Elephants now trundle,
The Lions ate their Tamer,
  And went back to the jungle.

Across the open seas,
  By no man seen today,
Through waves and ocean swell,
  The Sea Lions swim and play.

You'll find the humpback Camels,
  Back in their desert home,
A life's desire fulfilled,
  Across the sands to roam.

Those enigmatic Clowns,
Have sprung their last surprise,
The Tall Man left his stilts,
And is down to normal size.

Brave Acrobats and Tumblers,
Will find no work today,
Floodlights and equipment,
Are long since stored away.

Now the Park is empty,
Grass grows undisturbed,
The only sound we hear,
A sad song from a bird.

Yet we'll remember with affection,
In another time and place,
The magic of the Sawdust Ring,
Which nothing can replace.

In those happy days of childhood,
We never wore a frown,
For our hearts were filled with joy,
When the Circus came to Town.

A GRUESOME EXPERIENCE

With deep foreboding, we journeyed into the abyss,
  Would we take fright,
  At a noise in the night,
Were there Monsters and Ghouls in that darkness?

A scream greeted us, as we rounded a bend,
  Where a gruesome old face,
  On a sheet of white lace,
Gave a shudder, and our hair stood on end.

Strange gossamer cobwebs, our faces could feel,
  As the air turned much colder,
  Something tapped on our shoulders,
With frozen fingers, heavy as steel.

Some rattling chains, a moan and a groan,
  Getting closer each minute,
  With no escape from it,
Oh, how we wished we were safely back home.

That splash in a pool, made us feel most unsteady,
  Would we plunge in,
  For an unwanted swim,
And be gulped by a creature, with jaws open ready?

Something feathery and large flapped near to our ears,
  As we brushed it aside,
  A door opened wide,
And the daylight spilled in, to allay all our fears.

In the welcoming sunshine, our heads still spun round,
  Yes, we held good and tight,
  And cried with delight,
On the Ghost Train, at the seaside Fairground.

MY DAILY SWIM

Adorned with cap and flippers,
I eagerly wade in,
To undertake the challenge,
Of my daily swim.

Seagulls sweep above me,
I hear their mournful cry,
An orange sun beats down,
From a cloudless sky.

In the tepid waters,
All hazards I ignore,
For my ultimate objective,
Is to reach the distant shore.

A friendly humpback whale,
Floats perilously near,
Spouting jets of water,
High into the air.

Foaming waves are rising,
Above my line of sight,
Tumbling down in torrents,
Shutting out the light.

Past a tiny island,
  Where noisy seals bask,
No time to pause until,
  I've carried through my task.

Inviting sandy beaches,
  Palm trees slim and tall,
Draw slowly into view,
  As my strength begins to pall.

With stiff and aching muscles,
  I haul myself ashore,
Thankful to have mastered,
  The elements once more.

Back on 'terra firma',
  Gratefully I rest,
Yet when tomorrow dawns,
  I'll begin another quest.

For a feeling of elation,
  Comes o'er me when I enter:
This *Indoor Tropical Paradise*,
At my *Modern Leisure Centre*.

A COOKERY LESSON

I took up cooking recently,
At my local college,
Of 'cordon bleu' I'd hoped,
To gain some useful knowledge.

In snow-white cap and apron,
I really looked the part,
And when teacher had arrived,
It was time to make a start.

My trials were successful,
With very few mistakes,
Until I tried a recipe,
Described as 'rock bun' cakes.

Combining the ingredients,
Was quite an undertaking,
But finally the mixture,
Was well prepared for baking.

I confidently hoped,
These confections would be tasty,
Then decided later on,
I might have been too hasty.

When a smell of 'something burning',
  Drifted round the room,
It seemed, within the oven,
  My buns had met their doom.

Filled with apprehension,
  I pulled ajar the door,
But in the hazy smoke,
  Visibility was poor.

My cakes had set like concrete,
  Not what I'd really meant,
They resembled lumps of coal,
  And tasted like cement.

For that culinary blunder,
  I proffered no excuse,
As my humble little 'rockies',
  Now have another use.

I've informed my cookery teacher,
  — If she'll beg my pardon —
Having long desired a rockery,
  I've assigned them to the garden!

CAMEL RIDE

The camel train is ready,
For a journey, who knows where,
They scramble to their feet,
And we rise into the air.

On comfortable saddles,
Of blankets, made by hand,
We sway aboard the Dromedaries,
As they stride across the land.

We pass exotic species,
Of rainbow feathered birds,
And motley coloured animals,
Who graze in restless herds.

Upon the gentle breeze,
Come unfamiliar sounds,
Whilst something hurries by,
In furious leaps and bounds.

From realms of lions and tigers,
Growling fiercely,
To where the noonday sun,
Beats down relentlessly.

On to a green oasis,
With glistening pool and trees,
Where gratefully our mounts,
Sink down upon their knees.

Thus rested and refreshed,
The homeward trail we face,
Then eagerly the camels,
Quicken up the pace.

A summertime adventure,
Just made for me and you,
So we're off to see the world —
And it's once more round the Zoo!

WHITE HORSES

I sit and watch for hours,
  But approach them do not dare,
These beautiful white horses,
  As they gallop free as air.

With tails swishing fiercely,
  Eyes piercing, nostrils wide,
Outpacing one another,
  They demonstrate their pride.

Yet while I contemplate,
  What can they really be,
Nature illustrates,
  Her harsh reality.

For manes are silver foam,
  And not one horse is named,
They wear no bit and bridle,
  Thus never can be tamed.

Their brief lives will allow,
  No time for hesitation,
When brought vividly to life,
  By my imagination.

So, across the angry seas,
  Midst tumult and commotion,
They prance and dance — then disappear,
  Into the stormy ocean.

CARDBOARD TREES

The sun illuminates a clear blue sky,
As morning slowly breaks, the sleepy world awakes,
And for this tiny village day is nigh.

Down on the farm brown cows chew on hay,
Whilst eager collies creep, round wary flocks of sheep,
To bring them home from hillsides far away.

Before the plough a shire-horse makes his way,
Past weeping willow trees, swaying in the breeze,
Besides a pond, where ducklings swim and play.

A goods train skirts a mountain tall and stark,
And on its lonely route, gives a mournful hoot,
Then rolls into a tunnel gaunt and dark.

Noisy racing cars speed round a track,
On and on they go, swaying to and fro,
Till chequered flags wave the winners back.

*   *   *

Yet as we contemplate this scene, somehow,
It fades before our eyes, until we realise,
'Twas long ago, and life is different now.

For shadows of the evening fall at last,
And many a ghostly sound, reverberates around,
Of children's voices, echoing from the past.

Passing years have closed the farmyard gate,
And so this place of joy, for many a girl and boy,
Is thus abandoned to an unknown fate.

Now, wooden cows gaze at a tinfoil lake,
On the village green, the only movement seen,
Some cardboard trees, whose branches gently shake.

Woolly sheep are balls of nylon fur,
The collies, moving not, are frozen to the spot,
Painted mountains — but a distant blur.

This plaster horse stands stiffly by the door,
Its legs will never bend, the plough is just pretend,
For making furrows on the playroom floor.

No-one winds the clockwork train, alack,
No journey can it start, with rails bent apart,
Next to broken cars on plastic track.

Of these toys the children took their fill,
Now they've grown and gone, yet memories linger on,
And in the silent nursery, time stands still.

TELEVISION REPAIR

We called the TV man,
Just the other week,
As reception on our set,
Was really rather meek.

In fact it wasn't there at all,
No picture and no sound,
So he had to take the back off,
To have a look around.

Out came yards of wiring,
Reaching to the door,
With various bits and pieces,
Cluttering up the floor.

For many hours he struggled,
Trying to find the cause,
Daytime turned to evening,
But still he didn't pause.

"I hope you realise,"
He told us 'on the line',
"Outside normal hours,
I'm charging double time."

As night elapsed we knew,
His invoice would be vast,
So all our lifetime savings,
Were disappearing fast.

And just as we decided,
To call a final halt,
The set burst into life,
At last! he'd found the fault.

Then he told us something,
Not exactly funny,
One thing we'd overlooked,
Had cost us all our money.

The truth was very simple,
But hit us like a rocket —
That the TV works much better,
When *plugged into the socket!*

WAGON TRAIN

I rode my old brown mule Chinook,
Along a dusty trail one day,
Where, to my great bewilderment,
A Wagon Train rolled on its way.

Its herd of lowing cattle,
Took many hours to pass me by,
Whilst cowboys who were slumped on saddles,
Uttered many a weary sigh.

It trundled on through valleys,
O'er endless plains devoid of trees,
Where purple sage-brush nodded,
Fanned by a desert breeze.

As evening shadows lengthened,
The wagons pulled into a town,
The herd was calmed, and tired horses,
Watered, fed and bedded down.

Cowboys gambled with the dice,
Inside a brightly lit saloon,
A stagecoach clattered into view,
Silhouetted by the moon.

Eventually the noise abated,
Darkness soon eclipsed the light,
I crept away, unseen, unheard,
The town was sleeping for the night.

* * *

A few days later I set out,
To try and bring to life again,
My image of the West long past,
Projected by that Wagon Train.

The old saloon stood silent now,
All the wells were long since dry,
The buildings derelict and dark,
With ceilings open to the sky.

Of cattle, horses, cowboys brave,
The only traces to be found,
Some broken wheels, a rusty gun,
And hoofprints etched into the ground.

An old coyote howls alone,
Atop a melancholy hill,
And far across the lonesome prairie,
A Ghost Town keeps its secret still.

A NEW EXTENSION

When walking by my house,
Please notice as you pass,
I have a new extension,
To give a touch of class.

The craftsmen laboured hard,
With great alacrity,
They realised the building,
Deserved priority.

Brickie, joiner, plasterer,
Worked hard 'by the book',
The skilful decorator,
Achieved a 'finished' look.

The interior is filled,
With various 'objets d'art',
And there's a special area,
For meals 'a la carte'.

Furniture and fittings,
Give it a homely charm,
And a central heating radiator,
Will keep the inmate warm.

There's carpet wall-to-wall,
Of shag-pile, patterned grey,
The window's double glazed,
To scare Jack Frost away.

Although it cost a fortune,
I don't mind in the least,
The occupant-to-be,
Deserves the very best.

So all-in-all I hope,
After all this time and trouble,
My Puppy will be happy —
In his brand-new Kennel!

DOWN THE FAIRWAY

Upon a tee the golf ball quietly lies,
  My stance is '*de rigueur*',
  I take a swing with vigour,
Then down the fairway straight and true it flies.

Into the swirling mist with all its might,
  The small speck disappears,
  And all my hopes and fears,
Are centred on a flag, far out of sight.

With a bag of 'woods and irons' on my back,
  Towards the second tee,
  Wondering what I'll see,
I hasten down the well-worn sandy track.

Alas, there is no sign of my golf ball,
  And in the 'rough' for hours,
  Midst bushes, trees and flowers,
I search in vain, till evening shadows fall.

The 'Pro' gives me instructions and commands,
  Yet records sadly show,
  My golf balls usually go,
Where they carefully place the bunkers full of sand.

And, as I take another careful putt,
  Rain descends in sheets,
  Where no shelter is in reach,
Now I'm cold and wet from head to foot.

With great relief I reach the eighteenth green,
  My limbs are stiff and sore,
  So now I feel quite sure,
Of such exhausting games, enough I've seen.

Thus, on these Municipal Links down by the sea,
  As I struggle with my 'swing',
  Warning bells now ring,
That this game of 'PITCH & PUTT' — is too strenuous for me!

BR

It's early in the morning,
   And rush hour's under way,
As the busy Railway faces,
   Another hectic day.

Passengers are issued,
   With tickets for their ride,
Across the numerous platforms,
   Suitcase trolleys glide.

Sacks of mail and parcels,
   Arriving at the Station,
Soon will be transported,
   To distant destinations.

The Signalman observes,
   From his 'eyrie' high,
Which points need aligning,
   For each train passing by.

Periodic maintenance,
   Is carried out with care,
Ensuring miles of tracks,
   Are kept in good repair.

Goods trains trundle on,
   With loads of coal or grain,
Slowly up the gradients,
   While 'sleepers' take the strain.

O'er the countryside,
  Roars a lone express,
This 'Inter-City' special,
  Will be on time, no less.

The day progresses quickly,
  With no time for reflection,
Those homeward bound commuters,
  Must catch their last connection.

Slowly to the sidings,
  Glides a late night train,
Until a new dawn calls it,
  Into service once again.

Uniforms and flags,
  Are safely stored away,
The whistles of the Guards,
  Will sound no more today.

And, as evening closes in,
  I'm so loathe to depart,
From my Model Railway,
  Where I'm just a child at heart.

THE WEATHER-VANE

High above the countryside,
  A handsome fellow sways,
Atop a Church's spire,
  To mark the passing days.

He's but a lowly cockerel,
  Yet his joy he cannot hide,
As this important task,
  He carries out with pride.

Life presents no problems,
  His needs are very few,
A humble perch his home,
  With a panoramic view.

And he is never lonely,
  For each day brings a smile,
When his many feathered cousins,
  Pause to chat a while.

A sentry of the universe,
  While seasons come and go,
Faithfully watching over us,
  Through sunshine, rain or snow.

He keeps his silent vigil,
Far above the land,
Where he is one step nearer,
Heaven's welcome hand.

How I envy that young bird,
As I sadly look around,
At the hustle and the bustle,
Of life here on the ground.

And I'm sure I'll have a choice,
On what will be my fate,
When I visit earth again,
At a future date.

So, if you spot a weather-vane,
On a steeple in the sky,
It could be my next appearance,
In this world, by and by.

THE ALPHABET RACE

Albert was a bookworm,
Brave and ruthlessly,

Chewing through a race,
Down the dictionary,

Eager to do well,
Frantic to be seen,

Gradually outpacing,
His opponents, keen,

Inching to the lead,
Jauntily and able,

Keeping powerful jaws,
Loose and pliable,

Master at the half-way stage,
No time did he waste,

Overtook his rivals,
Panting with the pace,

Quickening the rhythm,
Resting not at all,

Stamina was vital,
To earn the ultimate goal,

Upon the final section,
Victory was sighted,

Within the great book's pages,
X-rays showed, highlighted,

Yes, the race was won, for at
ZERO he'd alighted!

MY MAN

Handsome in his overcoat,
  And trilby hat of grey,
With woolly gloves and scarf,
  My man was there each day.

A smile adorned his face,
  For those who came to call,
Children, birds and animals,
  Were greeted one and all.

Puffing on a briar pipe,
  He looked so fit and well,
But just how long he'd stay,
  Only time would tell.

For milder days of Spring,
  Across the landscape loomed,
Thus to depart with haste,
  My man was surely doomed.

One night a storm blew up,
  For many hours it rained,
And in the early morning,
  No sign of him remained.

My talents could not save him,
  Albeit I'm quite clever,
For now the Winter's over,
  And my Snowman's gone for ever.

LODGERS

There is another family,
  Sharing our home today,
They moved in unexpectedly,
  Whilst we were away.

We attempted to persuade them,
  To try some other town,
But all our efforts failed,
  And they happily settled down.

Their needs are very simple,
  Just regular meals will please,
Plus a warm and comfy bedroom,
  In which to take their ease.

We hardly ever see them,
  As they quietly come and go,
Perhaps in early evening,
  They'll call to say 'hello'.

The youngsters enjoy playing,
  When no-one is around,
But if someone appears,
  To Mum and Dad they bound.

Although we quite enjoy,
Their geniality,
Sometimes they take advantage,
Of our hospitality.

In the early hours,
Whilst we are asleep,
With a moonlit feast in mind,
To the larder they all creep.

And lately we have noticed,
They seem to have no qualms,
About a rummage in our wardrobes,
Seeking clothing nice and warm.

Yet frankly we confess,
For the sake of harmony,
We overlook these misdemeanours,
And enjoy their company.

So we say 'goodnight' each evening,
As we close the parlour door,
To Mister Mouse and Mistress Mouse,
Plus their children — four.

BABY-SITTING

Tonight I'm baby-sitting,
An easy task I'd say,
I'm sure my little charges,
Will dream the hours away.

My friends have reassured me,
The youngsters will not stir,
So gratefully I sink,
Into a deep armchair.

Alas, my short siesta,
Is shattered suddenly,
By a loud commotion,
From the nursery.

With some trepidation,
I peer in through the door,
To see a scene of chaos,
Spread across the floor.

To calm the active duo,
I frantically try,
As blankets, cushions, pillows,
All around me fly.

It seems the young ones feel,
As they tumble with delight,
The time for fun and games,
Is the middle of the night.

Quickly to the kitchen,
They follow me with glee,
Where a soothing drink,
Quells all activity.

Thus settled in their beds,
Two sleepy heads now lie,
And in the easy chair,
I slump with one big sigh.

From their evening out,
My friends arrive home early,
Anxious that their little ones,
Are still content and comfy.

Little do they know,
What disruption there has been,
Whilst happily they gaze,
Upon this peaceful scene.

For, after just one bark,
And a faint miaow,
The Puppy and the Kitten,
Are sleeping soundly now!

RELUCTANT HERO

I donned my climbing gear,
For the great ascent,
With nylon ropes and crampons,
To succeed was my intent.

At first it was quite easy,
My heart was set aglow,
With voices of encouragement,
Echoing from below.

But as I clambered upwards,
Being careful not to fall,
My brief enthusiasm,
Soon began to pall.

The wind was howling loudly,
I perilously swayed,
And all around my face,
Silent snowflakes played.

From my ears hung icicles,
Hands were raw and cold,
I blindly groped about,
Searching for a hold.

In the upper atmosphere,
The air was rather thin,
When I gasped for breath,
My vision grew more dim.

Soon my clothes were tattered,
As the climb became too rough,
I'm sure that scaling 'Everest',
Isn't half as tough.

A massive Golden Eagle,
'Buzzed' me from its eyrie,
Whilst I scrambled to the summit,
Extremely tired and weary.

Mission all completed,
I quickly turned around,
And with a safe descent,
Finally reached the ground.

So, although my friends cried 'Hero',
And waved aloft their hats,
That's the last time I climb *trees*
— to rescue stranded Cats!

MY NEW INVENTION

I am a great inventor,
Of fine machinery,
    Which, for anyone who asks,
    Will perform enormous tasks,
With adept efficiency.

With overall approval,
For my latest robot grand,
    Of intricate design,
    And workmanship so fine,
I'd have the world at my command.

Among its range of uses,
It digs holes large and small,
    Can lift a ton or more,
    Through concrete quickly bore,
And will even build a wall.

Path and roads it clears,
Of Autumn leaves, or snow,
    It prunes all trees and shrubs,
    And plants up garden tubs,
To make a Summer show.

It will wash and iron clothes,
Lay the table with a flourish,
    Take the dog a walk,
    In the local park,
Then give the car a polish.

*   *   *

Then one day a competition,
For talent such as mine,
    Was nearby taking place,
    To find the best device,
Which justified acclaim.

So I took my masterpiece,
To have its talents rated,
  By the experts who,
  Know a thing or two,
About gadgets automated.

The tests and trials were many,
For it to undertake,
  Thus at the big convention,
  Where I entered this invention,
My reputation was at stake.

As they pressed its switches,
It keenly set to work,
  And most impressively,
  Buzzed obediently,
Thus no order did it shirk.

My remarkable contraption,
Performed with expertise,
  Parachutes it stitched,
  Cricket balls it pitched,
All with the greatest ease.

Yet, sadly to relate,
A simple situation,
  Vital to us all,
  Became its big downfall,
When it fluffed one operation.

I'd hoped it would achieve,
The top award for me,
  But hearts it did not win,
  As it would not programme in,
— To make a cup of tea!

TEN POUNDS

The final decision was made,
Our passages booked and paid,
  Belongings were in a neat pack,
  By then there was no turning back.

They asked for volunteers who,
Would see a journey through,
  To a country knowing no bounds,
  For the price of hope — and ten pounds.

An Odyssey we thought would be,
A great opportunity,
  For seeking adventures galore,
  When we reached that distant shore.

As we bid a final farewell,
To family and friends, none could tell,
  If we'd ever see them again,
  Or would only memories remain?

But we knew we could always dream,
Of the tiny babbling stream,
  Which carefully threads its way,
  Through the woods where we used to play.

And the same sun and moon were in sight,
To illuminate each day and night,
  Where half-way around the world,
  We might see a new life unfurled.

Our homeland slipped past with the miles,
We put on our bravest smiles,
  Yet when the port came in view,
  Our hearts missed a beat or two.

Thus we heard the ominous wail,
From a great ship waiting to sail,
  And answered its beckoning sound,
  — For we were Australia bound.

BEING POORLY

Try and enjoy being poorly,
  Make the best of it all while you may,
It's the only time all the attention,
  Is focused on you day by day.

Everyone's sending you cards,
  Plus bunches of flowers and grapes,
You've discovered the secret of sympathy,
  Just a few coughs and groans is all it takes.

I've taken a full week off work,
  To care for you all of the while,
I'll know that my efforts are worth it,
  If occasionally you give me a smile.

The TV is at your disposal,
  Plus magazines and books to digest,
With the radio placed within reach,
  This leisurely life is the best.

Your bed has been made, pillows plumped,
  With you still ensconed, lying prone,
For once the household routine,
  Is centred on just you alone.

And I've tramped up those stairs all day long,
  Carrying a tray in my hand,
With assortments of sandwiches and cakes,
  Plus a mug of clear soup, warm and bland.

Hour by hour you're gradually improving,
  By the glint in your eyes I can tell,
So try and enjoy being poorly,
  For there'll be no more of this — once you're well!

MOVING HOUSE

A considerable upheaval,
Saw us moving house today,
  In the mists of early morning,
  We slowly made our way,
Across the country wide,
Where our destination lay.

In wooden crates and boxes,
Crockery was stacked,
  Clothes and favourite books,
  In large suitcases packed,
Whilst underlay and carpets,
Were rolled and tightly wrapped.

Five hundred miles we covered,
Our major motivation —
  A new home to relax in,
  Thus with grateful expectation,
Feeling tired and weary,
We reached our destination.

From our laden motor car,
And two removal vans,
  Furniture and chattels,
  Were unloaded by all hands,
Yet tonight in desolation,
Our cottage empty stands.

Due to an oversight,
Of an unexpected kind,
  We're camping in the garden,
  As, despondently we find,
In all the hustle-bustle,
— We left the key behind.

AN EXCITING FIND

We wanted to be famous, someone of eminence,
So took up archaeology, our own 'dig' to commence.

At a likely spot across a grassy field,
We started excavations, to see what it would yield.

Several days we toiled, the hole increased in size,
We'd almost given up hope, when much to our surprise.

Embedded in the ground, our spades unearthed some bones,
With bated breath we gently moved away the stones.

Could there be a Dinosaur buried deep below?
Which once patrolled the earth, several million years ago.

We wondered as we burrowed, what we might find next,
Perhaps a Brontosaurus, or the mighty famed 'T. Rex'.

Maybe this was the chance of which we always dreamed,
The experts would soon tell us if all was what it seemed.

But sadly to relate our hopes began to fade,
When a close examination of the bones was made.

"They're not quite old enough" the experts pointed out,
"All that time ago, not much plastic was about."

And our claim to fame diminished, just as we had feared,
When underneath the microscope, some wording soon appeared.

Etched upon the skeleton, the truth spread out before us,
'Twas not an extinct species; but a 'MADE-IN-BRITAINSAURUS'.

A HAIRY DO

Unkempt my hair was looking,
 And very much neglected,
So I visited the stylist,
 To have it resurrected.

I asked for something modern,
 To give my locks a glow,
A simple curly 'perm',
 Or perhaps just 'cut and blow'.

With an air of reassurance,
 That it would be OK,
They keenly set about it,
 In a most determined way.

Through the day they toiled,
 The hours crept slowly past,
When from beneath the dryer,
 I emerged at last.

Gazing in the mirror,
 I saw to my dismay,
Those once dull tresses, now,
 Were a dazzling display.

My hair was brightly tinted,
  With rainbow coloured stripes,
And stiffly overhead,
  Was standing up in spikes.

"This is the latest fashion,"
  They hastily explained,
As, of my former style,
  Nothing now remained.

Yet, still I am undaunted,
  In spite of all these trials,
For when I least expect it,
  Fortune often smiles.

And there's an opportunity,
  For exhibiting my 'crown',
In a grand procession,
  Tomorrow through the town.

I won't need fancy dress,
  With my hair of every shade,
To be the star attraction,
  In the Carnival Parade!

SCHOOL

It's Monday once again,
The weekend homework's done,
Today a History lesson,
'Just who was that King's son?'

Tuesday sees me frantic,
For recipes I'm looking,
To take to 'Household Management',
(To us that's plain old 'Cooking'.)

Wednesday I enjoy, as,
In the 'Gym' we're all let loose,
Where benches, ropes and wall-bars,
Are put to fullest use.

That dreaded word 'Mathematics',
Looms ominously high,
Oh! how I wish that Thursday,
Would quickly pass me by.

On Friday, 'English Literature',
Completes the week's routines,
But will I ever understand,
Exactly what it means?

Neither Saturday nor Sunday,
  Can I enjoy myself,
I have to study thoroughly,
  Those books upon the shelf.

That I'll be very clever,
  There really is no doubt,
But my world outside the classroom,
  Is gradually losing out.

All this education,
  Has brought me to my knees,
And someone who has noticed,
  Is feeling none too pleased.

So I'll have to give up work,
  As time too swiftly passes,
For my boss says I'm worn out,
  Attending 'Evening Classes'.

A SPENDING SPREE

I've just been on a 'spending spree',
To the busy city,
Although there is a dearth,
Of funds within my 'kitty'.

A 3-piece suite of furniture,
Made an excellent start,
Plus a cooker for the kitchen,
To put me in great heart.

At the fashion shop,
I pondered for a while,
Before I chose new outfits,
Which really suit my style.

From the garden centre,
To keep my grass quite neat,
A motorized lawn-mower,
Complete with driver's seat.

Of new cars in a show-room,
My selection made today,
Is the latest streamlined model,
In a pleasant shade of grey.

Curtains for the windows,
  Mirrors for the hall,
A decorative tea service,
  Of finest quality all.

So, if you wonder how I'm able,
  These luxuries to buy,
Whilst spending very little,
  Here's the reason why.

I never take a cheque book,
  Or fancy plastic card,
My purse is almost empty,
  Yet paying is not hard.

Because, I don't need money,
  When round the stores I'm hopping,
As, it doesn't cost a lot,
  Going 'Window Shopping'.

CONSTRUCTIONAL ENGINEER

A builder of repute I claim to be,
  Of the highest grade,
  Perfection in the trade,
My workmanship is excellent, you'll agree.

Yet I admit to having one downfall,
  Speed is not my style,
  So it takes a while,
For any job to reach its final call.

With all the struggle giving of my best,
  I deserve a little break,
  So an effort I will make,
To leave the work in hand, and take a rest.

Folks who know me never make a fuss,
  When a project may,
  Be subject to delay,
They know it will be finished in due course.

I go the speed which suits my inclination,
  As, no-one's in a race,
  To occupy the place,
For this house, there is no desperation.

Thus another year slips quietly past,
  Until one day I feel,
  My enthusiasm's real,
And to task in hand I turn at last.

So if you wonder why I build in snatches,
  The reason is quite clear,
  I'm a model engineer,
And my construction's merely *glue* and *matches*.

NATURE'S GARDEN

My cottage garden border,
  Was looking rather sorry,
So I placed a seedling order,
  With my local Nursery.

Parcels soon arrived,
  Of seeds for cultivation,
Which patiently I strived,
  To sow with dedication.

Shortly, tiny shoots,
  Appeared within my bower,
Spreading out their roots,
  To feed each growing flower.

Yet, blossoms there assembled,
  To my consternation,
Did not quite resemble,
  The catalogue illustrations.

They came up quite informally,
  Spreading all around,
Plants which are not normally,
  Found on tended ground.

A sign to me that Nature,
  Displays the wisest deeds,
And will not copy pictures,
  Adorning packs of seeds.

So, with Her own selection,
  In a blaze of colours grand,
I have the best collection,
  Of wild flowers, in the land.

THIS DAY

Six o'clock this morning,
  Sunshine slowly breaks,
Through the early mist,
  As the world awakes.

Tramcars clatter by,
  And workers make their way,
To factories and mills,
  For another day.

A dust-cart rumbles on,
  Pulled by an old brown mare,
Retirement's imminent,
  Green pastures wait for her.

Ladies in long dresses,
  Sweeping o'er the ground,
Crossing dusty streets,
  To local shops are bound.

A pony leaves its stable,
  For harnessing once more,
To the family trap,
  For its daily chore.

From the railway station,
 Slowly moves a train,
The engine steams and snorts,
 As it takes the strain.

Down the slim canal,
 Across the country wide,
Heavily laden barges,
 In eerie silence glide.

Only flickering gas lamps,
 Line the cobbled lanes,
Where children in their clogs,
 Play mysterious games.

Yet these strange events,
 We do not witness now,
So it's hard to comprehend,
 They did exist somehow.

They are not merely day-dreams,
 But happened once, you know,
As told in someone's diary,
 From long, long ago.

LUNCH-TIME

The day was warm and sunny,
  I heard the singing of a lark,
So headed to the countryside,
  For a summer walk.

Over hills and valleys,
  I tramped for many miles,
Till stiffness and fatigue,
  Dampened down my smiles.

To boost my flagging strength,
  Some nourishment was due,
But in that barren landscape,
  Nowhere was in view.

Then I reached a crest,
  My heart was set aglow,
A tiny village stood,
  In the vale below.

To cure my thirst and hunger,
  And ease my aching feet,
I sought a place to rest,
  Along its narrow street.

A welcome sign marked 'Cafe',
   Adorned a tiny store,
With my final ounce of strength,
   I limped a few yards more.

Displayed outside the building,
   In letters large and clear,
Were the cheering words,
   'We serve refreshments here'.

Soon I could relax,
   In a comfy chair,
With a soothing drink,
   To banish every care.

Alas, my hopes were dashed,
   Of something good to munch,
As, a sign upon the door read:—
   '*Sorry, gone to lunch*'.

AWASH!

The ferry boat awaits,
  For passengers to board,
With a busy schedule,
  Lost time it can't afford.

A rugged rope uncoils,
  From its capstan's grip,
Everyone prepares,
  For a pleasant trip.

Slowly out of dock,
  The ship glides cautiously,
Ahead the open ocean,
  Tumbles restlessly.

Stormy looking clouds,
  Ominously grey,
Gather far above,
  The vessel starts to sway.

Into his telescope,
  The Captain grimly peers,
His face is white and gaunt,
  For a sudden squall he fears.

Waves of silver foam,
   Rise mercilessly high,
With unremitting strength,
   Blotting out the sky.

The sun sinks out of sight,
   As the gale increases,
Everyone turns green,
   All conversation ceases.

After drifting many hours,
   At the sea's command,
Just when hope is fading,
   Someone spots the land.

At last the port is reached,
   The ship is safe once more,
And everyone is guided,
   Safely back ashore.

So ends another voyage,
   — Must put the toys away,
Now that bath time's over,
   For another day!

BACK IN FASHION

In a bygone age,
My clothes were all the rage,
I proudly wore the latest trend each year,
But as the time goes by,
No matter how I try,
I cannot keep abreast with modern 'gear'.

Of fashion sense as such,
I've lost that magic touch,
My current 'dress' is sadly out-of-date,
And on the rare occasion,
When I buy a new creation,
The choice is left entirely up to fate.

Although no longer smart,
Still I will not part,
With favourite outfits from my vibrant youth,
They hang upon a rail,
Looking sad and pale,
And patiently await their 'day of truth'.

Yet, as the wise men say,
"To everything its day,"
And nothing's really new, I now discern,
My eagerness to hoard,
Will bring its own reward,
For the styles within my wardrobe will return.

Thus, smothered in moth-balls,
Come two-piece suits and shawls,
Some to be flaunted by the 'younger set',
So after decades three or four,
The circle turns once more,
And I'll be back in fashion even yet!

SNOOKERED

The Snooker season's finally over,
And stars are resting out at clover,
  You've put the TV set to bed,
  As Summer months now loom ahead.

Snooker balls of many hues,
Struck by a hundred eager cues,
  Into the six awaiting pockets,
  Slowly rolled, or sped like rockets.

Rivals played their final scene,
Now you reflect what might have been,
  Yet if your favourite lost once more,
  He'll try next year, you can be sure.

Of such excitement you've had enough,
For an avid Snooker buff,
  It only causes you to shake,
  To see a one-four-seven break.

Be brave, remember when you're able,
You'll see a light beyond that 'Table',
  As other entertainments may,
  Help you pass the time away.

And soon the day will come around,
When Autumn leaves float to the ground,
  Then once again we'll hear you cheer,
  "Another Snooker season's here."

DRIVING TEST

I had to take my driving test,
Just the other day,
So with keen determination,
To the Centre made my way.

As I slipped the car in gear,
And cautiously set out,
Of my ultimate success,
I really had no doubt.

The first few miles were easy,
Mistakes I made were few,
Which assured the man besides me,
A good test was in view.

But soon my 'lefts' and 'rights',
Were becoming all confused,
Yet to give up in mid-stream,
I fervently refused.

Along a one-way street,
I puzzle to this day,
Why the other traffic,
Was going the opposite way.

While reversing round a corner,
I was rather wide again,
Which left us badly stranded,
On the wrong side of the lane.

And propulsion from my hill start,
   Did not take us far,
As we gently travelled backwards,
   Into another car.

Stopping in emergency,
   I carried out with zest,
Although 'twas almost half-a-mile,
   Before we came to rest.

Yet in spite of these shortcomings,
   When my driving was inspected,
I passed with 'flying colours',
   Exactly as expected.

So with only you alone,
   This secret I will share,
Why my benevolent passenger,
   To fail me did not dare.

I had a genuine reason,
   For that confidence and stamina,
Because —
   It was my HUSBAND, who was the Test Examiner.

THE OLD-TIMER

Now aged a hundred years,
  Life to him is good,
In the countryside, his home,
  Besides a leafy wood.

Many are the friends,
  Who visit him each day,
And children wave a greeting,
  When they run past to play.

A grassy field his bed,
  His roof, the open sky,
From this proud domain,
  He sees the world go by.

Tiny woodland creatures,
  Keep him company,
As, with their daily tasks,
  He helps them, cheerfully.

The birds all love him dearly,
  And to each other call,
Perched upon his outstretched arms,
  With no fear at all.

He takes the Seasons in his stride,
As they come and go,
Warmth of the Summer's sun,
And chill of Winter's snow.

His clothes are few, but varied,
Yet he never wears them out,
A jacket light for Spring,
And warm brown Autumn coat.

With a minimum of effort,
He stills the hands of time,
So throughout the fleeting decades,
Remains within his prime.

And when this earth has said,
Goodbye to you and me,
He'll see another Century out,
— This sturdy old Oak-tree.

VISITING THE DENTIST

I rang the Dentist's bell, and was ushered to his 'lair',
Abruptly I was seated in the dreaded chair.

An overpowering arc light shone into my face,
He gathered up his tools, my heart began to race.

Instructions "open wide" boomed into my ears,
His grim determination did not allay my fears.

Protests went unheeded, and I finally had to yield,
As all routes of escape hastily were sealed.

"They'll have to be removed" was the awful verdict,
I slipped deep into sleep, as the gas soon took effect.

When I stirred, my mouth was devoid of all its teeth,
My tongue searched fruitlessly, for no molars lay beneath.

Towards the door I crept, in shock and indignation,
The Dentist called me back, for an explanation.

"Just a moment please" I heard him swiftly say,
"For professional services, my bill you'll have to pay."

"I didn't want your treatment" was my sad reply,
Bemused the Dentist asked me for a reason why.

I soon produced some evidence, that my visit was routine,
And I still might have my teeth, if he hadn't been so keen.

Thus apologies were offered, when he realised much later,
With my book and pen — I'd only gone to read the meter!

TO RUMMY

Thank you for the pleasure,
You gave us all,
  Your bravery and courage,
  We still recall.

Thirty famous fences,
Five times cleared,
  'The Chair' and daunting 'Bechers',
  You never feared.

A shout went up "Red Rum
Has won again",
  A record third time brought you
  Worldwide fame.

Grand the 'National' is, but
Different now,
  Since from the race you took
  Your final bow.

Yet each year, amongst the runners
Keen and strong,
  Our imaginations see you
  Skip along.

Now, as a special tribute,
Your statue will
  Proudly stand at Aintree,
  To remind us still.

To you —
In your comfortable stable,
Where you spend
  Your happy retirement,
  — Our love we send.

DIY

The country's favourite hobby is 'Doing-It-Yourself',
So I thought I'd be a handyman and try it for myself.
With suitable materials, just think what I'd do then,
And save myself a fortune by not paying other men.

From the local library, with keen anticipation,
I borrowed various books of useful information.
It cost a small fortune for the right equipment,
I went home heavily laden, to start refurbishment.

The first job to be tackled was smartening up my hall,
With a shelf for chinaware, fixed upon the wall.
Later on alas, the shelf was on the ground,
With broken crockery fragments scattered all around.

Much time within the kitchen I would need to spend,
To replace corroded fittings and clear a blocked 'U' bend.
But before removing pipework, good care I did not take,
To turn the water off, soon the floor was like a lake.

Interior decorations should not take too long,
With tins of gloss and brushes, nothing could go wrong.
Eventually the woodwork was painted bright as new,
— Plus floors, walls, furniture, and my best clothing too!

Attention to the roof was needed urgently,
  I clambered to the apex and began work fervently.
Slates were carefully fixed atop the house so tall,
  When a force-ten gale arose, and groundward blew them all.

I'd tile the bathroom walls, that should be straightforward,
  But getting them in place proved to be quite awkward.
Whilst balancing aloft, from the steps I fell,
  Cracking all the tiles, and the bath as well.

At last the truth had dawned, I really could not win,
  The only real solution was to call the experts in.
Plumbers, Builders, Tilers, all of them were needed,
  If only their advice beforehand I had heeded.

Now my home is modernised in every single way,
  Yet I'll have to sell it soon, because of all the bills to pay.
So I've come to the conclusion, as I rue my missing wealth,
  I'm really not cut out for 'Doing-It-Myself'.

EMPTY BOXES

I sought an occupation,
  To fill my time each day,
So working in a toffee shop,
  Seemed the perfect way.

An ideal job was found,
  In a local store,
Selling tasty sweetmeats,
  I could not ask for more.

With a steady stream of sales,
  I must honestly confess,
The hectic early morning,
  Was a great success.

I took out folk's selections,
  Much to their delight,
From the well-filled shelves,
  In the window bright.

But the busy afternoon,
  Was interrupted by a roar,
From a crowd of irate customers,
  Clamouring at the door.

Clutching in their hands,
  Somewhat in disarray,
Purchases they'd made,
  Earlier in the day.

The candies they had bought,
  A few short hours ago,
Were totally inedible,
  They wanted me to know.

Were my gallant efforts,
  Too good to be true?
I'd sold the entire stock,
  So what more could I do?

'Twas then the boss revealed,
  The cause of my downfall,
The confections in the window,
  Were not for sale at all.

They were only for display,
  Just immitations plenty — as
All the sweets were plastic,
  And all the boxes empty!

THE HAUNTED MUSEUM

High upon a hilltop,
  Clothed in a misty shroud,
Stands the dour Museum,
  Like a Castle proud.

The oaken door was open,
  I eagerly strode through,
To see the ancient artifacts,
  Of history on view.

An Egyptian King's dark tomb,
  Was open to the sky,
On peering in I saw,
  His spectre floating by.

A painting of the Devil,
  In a gallery of blue,
His green eyes mesmerised me,
  As I tiptoed quickly through.

Statues of the Gods,
  From early Rome and Greece,
Breathed on my neck cold air,
  Sending shudders to my knees.

Why did the lights dim slowly,
  When I moved among old bones?
Creating ghostly shadows,
  Accompanied by low moans.

Gorgons on a Temple,
  Re-erected from afar,
How did the fearsome creatures,
  Leave on me a crimson scar?

That lion on a pillar,
  Its jaws were closed before,
When I glanced a second time,
  It gave a frightening roar.

From a re-created dungeon,
  Down musty cellar steps,
Some heavy iron chains,
  Rattled in the gloomy depths.

The halls and corridors,
   Seemed like a giant maze,
As I stumbled to the exit,
   Somewhat in a daze.

I left the daunting building,
   To breathe again fresh air,
And sped hastily away,
   Leaving many mysteries there.

Back to cheerful comforts,
   Of my familiar home,
Yet hidden voices told me,
   That I was not alone.

An unknown force which lived,
   Within those walls, may,
Have accompanied me out,
   On that fateful day.

Since my traumatic visit,
   Life is different here,
The house has come alive,
   With another presence near.

Lights switch on at random,
   During daylight hours,
My cleaner sweeps the carpets,
   Controlled by other powers.

Without my assistance,
   The radio changes band,
Curtains close and open,
   Via someone else's hand.

This invisible companion,
   Has taken full control,
Leaving me perplexed,
   In a secondary role.

So as I pause to ponder,
   A question haunts me still —
What alien spirits walk,
   The Museum on the hill?

COMFORTABLE SHOES

It was sale time at the shoe shop,
   And I needed a new pair,
So I joined the bargain hunters,
   At the footwear fair.

The latest fashions filled the store,
   Far as the eye could see,
But some to give me comfort,
   Were my priority.

Scores of people gathered,
   Round a well-filled shelf,
As I took my old ones off,
   To try some for myself.

Soon the floor was littered,
   With shoes of every kind,
Yet ones to suit me nicely,
   Were very hard to find.

The time had almost come,
   To beat a quick retreat,
When I grasped a final pair,
   And pulled them on my feet.

They fitted me like gloves,
   My agony was eased,
So I joined the 'pay here' queue,
   Feeling very pleased.

I paid the cashier gladly,
   It was my lucky day,
And wore my newest purchases,
   On the homeward way.

But a close examination,
   Made me feel distraught,
No wonder they felt comfy,
   — My own shoes I had bought!

ANOTHER POEM

"Not another poem" did I hear you say?
"At this frantic rate, there'll be one each day."

"Folks have bravely suffered, your rhymes for all these years,
They've only just perused some, when another one appears."

"At saturation point, it's time to take a bow,
And quietly change direction, you can do it now."

"As you've reached the fifty, the day has surely come,
To find another hobby, something much more fun."

"There's life beyond a notebook" I hear you telling me,
"Try and be an artist, and paint that yonder tree."

Yet in spite of your advice, I'm really on top form,
And heading for a century, so watch out now — be warned.

I know they're an encumbrance, but some day you'll find,
I'll be rich and famous, *then* you'll change your mind.

MY NEW CARPET

I had a brand-new carpet,
In lightest misty grey,
Fitted in my home,
Just the other day.

All the rooms were covered,
Plus Landing, Hall and Stair,
To keep it clean and fresh,
I treated it with care.

Then one stormy morning,
The door flew open wide,
And from the rain-soaked garden,
An 'army' marched inside.

Puppy-dogs and children,
With dirt up to their knees,
Filled the house in minutes,
As they flitted round like bees.

I gazed about astonished,
As, much to my distress,
The carpet was transformed,
To a muddy wilderness.

No amount of scrubbing,
Would remove a single streak,
A solution more dramatic,
I quickly had to seek.

Then I had a brainwave,
  And bought, without ado,
A pot of carpet dye,
  In deepest chocolate hue.

Into the tin of dye,
  Paws were gently dipped,
Then all around the house,
  The puppies gaily tripped.

And a hasty search revealed,
  Something else to use,
There within a cupboard,
  A pair of ancient shoes.

Soles were duly coated,
  And on the carpet neat,
I stepped with gay abandon,
  'Til the pattern was complete.

So I'll have no more worries,
  When there's heavy rain outdoors,
Pets' and people's feet marks,
  Won't show upon my floors.

My carpet's now my pride,
  In abstract grey and brown,
With 'Shoe and Paw' design,
  It's the envy of the town.

KNITTING

I was never a knitter,
   Of any renown,
   Poor results let me down,
And a pair of long needles,
   I viewed with a frown.

Of previous experience,
   With wool in a ball,
   All I recall,
Is playtime with kitten,
   Tying knots round us all.

Instructions and patterns,
   Were a puzzle to me,
   I just couldn't see,
How 'knit one' and 'purl two',
   Would be tackled with glee.

Yet that has all changed,
   And in the past year,
   Without any fear,
Striped scarves and bob hats,
   I now produce here.

Warm winter jumpers,
In yellows and blues,
Or mixed rainbow hues,
I make in abundance,
From which folk can choose.

My friends and relations,
Raise up a glass,
Yet cry out 'alas',
When more 'cabled V-necks',
I give them '*en masse*'.

So I'm warning you now,
My next gift to you,
Is long overdue,
Soon you'll find gloves and bedsocks,
In a parcel or two.

My redoubtable talent,
Is here to be seen,
I'm ever so keen,
And turn them out by the dozen,
On my *Knitting Machine!*

ALL-IN-ONE

There seems to be so many,
Holidays each year,
No sooner has one gone,
Than another will appear.

The Christmas season's over,
Then Easter time soon comes,
With fancy chocolate eggs,
And tasty hot cross buns.

Spring time then approaches,
Accompanied by the call:
'Bank Holidays are due,
We'll have to have them all.'

In the Summer months,
Folks are 'forced' to take,
At least a couple of weeks,
For their annual break.

Autumn time commences,
With yet another Monday,
When everyone looks forward,
To a final fun day.

Now the time has come,
These vacations to combine,
And have one long respite,
It will work out fine.

Next month has been selected,
For purely recreation,
And to start the holiday,
We'll have a celebration.

Therefore you are invited,
To be hale and hearty,
At our: Spring and Autumn,
Christmas/Easter,
Summer Garden Party!

A MOST UNUSUAL DAY

Something most unusual,
Has this day arisen,
Unexpected to us all,
No warnings were we given.

From normal hustle bustle,
Of a regular routine,
We see around the country,
A most chaotic scene.

Cars which yesterday,
Chugged merrily along,
Are now reluctant to begin,
Their engines' purring song.

Trains slow down as crews,
Can't quite believe their eyes,
British Rail has yet again,
Been taken by surprise.

The Airport's closed and silent,
No flights at all today,
Noisy giants are grounded, yet
We miss them in a way.

All schools are deserted,
Where children now should be,
In Parks there's only silence,
No wildlife there to see.

To shop is quite impossible,
The big stores wait in vain,
Customers don't venture out,
At home they all remain.

It'll take time to recover,
And get back into gear,
All because we've suddenly had —
The first snow of the year!

THE EMPEROR'S WARRIORS

Beneath the ancient earth,
Lost until our day,
Immortal Chinese Warriors,
Of Terracotta clay.

Within one fateful week,
A farmer's simple spade,
Plunged into the ground,
And this discovery made.

Seven thousand soldiers,
Armed with bows and spears,
Many hundred horses,
Buried all these years.

The Emperor's Warriors guarded,
His journey, strong and bold,
Towards an afterlife,
Along the unknown road.

Some men are standing proudly,
Or on one bended knee,
Ready for the conflict,
Which now will never be.

Each mighty muscled horse,
With square and stiffened jaw,
Eager for the gallop,
Now waits for evermore.

Carved in finest detail,
The craftsmen's skills unfurled,
Sets them amongst the greatest,
Wonders of the world.

And will this present age,
Seem strange and awesome whence,
Our secrets are uncovered,
Three thousand years hence.

A SPECIAL PRESENT

A rather special present,
 I've recently been given,
A splendid new typewriter,
 My spare time to enliven.

Its smart key-board is fitted,
 With every known device,
So sheets of correspondence,
 Are typed out in a trice.

I hoped it would be useful,
 For sending friends a letter,
At neatness and efficiency,
 Nothing could be better.

With envelopes and paper,
 I settled down to see,
If this clever instrument,
 Would be a help to me.

But sadly to relate,
 All is not quite right,
My machine does not perform,
 As I hoped it might.

It has a major problem,
 I tell you now directly:
'MY LUVLY KNEW TRIPEWRITER, CANOT SPEL CORECTLY!'

NATURE TRAIL

Nowhere can we find,
Enjoyment without fail,
Than a country walk,
Along the Nature Trail.

Creatures in abundance,
We can see right there,
Trees and plants and foliage,
Pleasures we all share.

Summer, Autumn, Winter,
Seasons ever changing,
Trees from bright Spring green,
To deeper emerald ranging.

Happy little animals,
Eye us curiously,
Rabbits, Badgers, Squirrels,
As they scurry tirelessly.

High up in the tree-tops,
Birds give out their song,
We glimpse fish in the river,
As they dart along.

Butterflies abound,
In many brilliant colours,
Sharing with the insects,
Bounty from the flowers.

Yet there is a puzzle,
On our rambles day or night,
Each year we observe,
Something's not quite right.

Movement is declining,
And slowly dawns the truth,
There's another species missing,
From the undergrowth.

Encroaching on their habitat,
  Come humans without pity,
Felling trees and hedges,
  For one more concrete city.

Nowhere left for digging,
  Burrows in the ground,
The birds cannot build nests,
  No branches to be found.

Streams and flowing rivers,
  Filled in and flattened over,
The swimming grounds are lost,
  To Otter, Fish and Beaver.

Now's the time to pause,
  And think for just a minute,
Do we need more land,
  To spread out to our limit?

When will we remember,
  As round about we roam,
The flowing stream and woodland,
  Is someone else's home.

We have to share the Earth,
  With our other friends,
Of fur and fin and feather,
  The World for all, God sends.

So we must never let,
  The awful day befall,
When we walk the Nature Trail,
  And nothing's there at all.

FREE COAL

Recently I started,
A job with 'National Coal',
I must say that the work,
Is pleasant on the whole.

But on arriving home,
Late the other day,
Right behind my house,
A ton of coal there lay.

It was, I understand,
Delivered by the 'Board',
Yet I received no warning,
Of this sudden hoard.

Their explanation is,
A big surprise to me,
"If you work for us,
We give you some coal free."

Rather like a colliery,
Now my garden looks,
People keep on calling,
To order winter stocks.

It smothers lawn and border,
Covering up my flowers,
Wherever can it go,
I ponder on for hours.

The mound is now extending,
Past my garden gate,
So there is just one answer,
Sadly to relate.

I'll have to give the job up,
Before life gets too hectic,
You see, the coal's no use to me,
Because I'm '*All Electric*'.

WAITING FOR A BUS

It's not a pleasant pastime,
  Waiting for a bus,
But as there is no option,
  I don't make a fuss.

Now I have been standing,
  Many hours in vain,
Without a 'mac' or 'brolly',
  In the pouring rain.

Though buses pass in dozens,
  Every hour each day,
When I really want one,
  Nothing comes my way.

On the wide horizon,
  Not one do I heed,
Just cars and trucks and lorries,
  Passing me at speed.

The time goes by so slowly,
  My legs and feet feel numb,
As I quietly contemplate,
  If one will ever come.

Shadows of the evening,
  Lengthen on the ground,
Folks who passed this morning,
  Now are homeward bound.

At last! a bus approaches,
  But it's no use you know,
Because — I've clean forgotten,
  Just where I want to go!

POOR OLD MILL

Poor old Mill,
  Standing all forlorn,
Abandoned and neglected,
  Your usefulness outworn.

Broken glass in windows,
  Frames devoid of paint,
Battered doors, rusty locks,
  In silence you wait.

No-one wants you now,
  The workers who once,
Filled you with sound,
  Of machinery and voice.

Now are gone forever,
  You did your best,
Producing bright cloth,
  Your looms now rest.

Is it goodbye?
  A last farewell,
Quickly to be pulled down,
  Your land will soon sell.

But that — was yesterday.

Now — a new morning,
Creeps through your door,
And what is happening?
People are here once more.

In overalls of blue and white,
Tools, paint and ladders tall,
Like busy bees,
Repairing chimney, roof and wall.

Your rooms are fitted out,
In brightly coloured ways,
Folks move in eagerly,
Gone are your lonely days.

Crafts of many kinds,
Artists, rooms of flowers,
Sounds of happy voices,
Will fill your hours.

Keenly you wait the opening,
Now you will,
Proudly greet your visitors,
Poor old happy Mill.

HIDDEN MEMORIES

Within the attic door,
  I turned a rusty key,
The hinges creaked and opened,
  What mysteries would I see?

Silken cobwebs hung,
  On gossamer-like strands,
Undisturbed for years,
  By any human hands.

Dusty packing cases,
  Filled with memories,
From another age,
  Of previous centuries.

A dappled rocking-horse,
  With tattered tail and mane,
Wooden-headed rag dolls,
  And broken clockwork train.

Books and faded letters,
  Along the years amassed,
And trunks of shabby clothing,
  Fashions of the past.

A box of faded photos,
  Someone's family,
No trace of who they were,
  Just part of history.

From the mists of ages,
The days had come alive,
Folks may come and go,
But artifacts survive.

Now I often think,
As I ponder to myself,
Although the past is over,
Will it repeat itself?

What of my possessions,
So modern bright and new,
Will a similar fate,
Overcome them too?

Yet I do not mind,
That a soul one day,
May find a little pleasure,
In a likewise way.

Let my own life be,
Placed safely into store,
Until another key,
Unlocks a secret door.

From attics of the future,
Will, I feel somehow,
Come someone gently smiling,
As I am smiling now.

SALE TIME

The Summer Sales are here,
Down town we made our way,
For a hectic day,
To see what special offers,
Within the big stores lay.

Shops were packed with thousands,
And in the milling throng,
We were transported along,
So to fill our bags to bursting,
Didn't take too long.

The rampant crowds rolled on,
Bumping arms and heads,
Clothing torn to shreds,
Buying all that came before us,
From 'candlesticks' to 'beds'.

Our purses soon looked thin,
Where did the money go?
We hadn't much to show,
As we slowly trundled homewards,
With our tales of woe.

And yet we never learn,
  It will only take a week,
  Until again we reach our peak,
Looking forward to the next Sales,
  When more bargains we will seek.

Now we're getting mobilised,
  For the next onslaught,
  This time we won't be caught,
There'll be no more cuts and bruises,
  We've protection of a sort.

We went to the Museum,
  And had a quiet word,
  When our story we proffered,
They loaned us two exhibits,
  Now we are prepared.

So, in heavy suits of armour,
  With vests of strong chain-mail,
  We'll be ready without fail,
For marching into combat,
  At the *January Sales!*

ONCE A SCARECROW

Once I was a scarecrow,
  In a field of corn,
With woolly scarf and gloves,
  To keep me nice and warm.

A tattered overcoat,
  And straw inside my boots,
Like a sentry guarding,
  The tiny growing shoots.

Birds they flocked in hundreds,
  To the farmer's field,
My job was to dissuade them,
  From eating all the yield.

Unfortunately a problem,
  Arose with me each day,
I hadn't got the heart,
  To scare the birds away.

They were so nice and friendly,
  And sang such happy songs,
Perched upon my shoulders,
  We were the best of friends.

Eventually the farmer,
  Told me I must go,
A scarecrow who loves birds,
  He didn't want to know.

I had to search for someone,
  To give a job to me,
But as a failed scarecrow,
  What use could I be?

At last some work I found,
  To fill me full of cheer,
You'll see me standing proudly,
  When you visit here.

I am amongst the birds,
  Whom I love the most,
And at the entrance gate,
  A signpost now I boast.

The message on it reads,
  In letters bright and new,

'OUR WILD BIRD SANCTUARY, HAS A WELCOME HERE FOR YOU.'

MIGRATING

I do not like the winter,
It holds no joy for me,
Somewhere warm and cosy,
I much prefer to be.

Lucky are the flocks of birds,
Which leave our shores each year,
For the warmer climates,
Of the Southern Hemisphere.

How I yearn to join them,
As they glide across the sky,
Yet with no wings or feathers,
I have no chance to fly.

But yes, there is an answer,
I've pondered long and hard,
Now something's taking shape,
In my own backyard.

I'll soon be floating with them,
To countries far away,
With seas of clearest blue,
And sunshine every day.

So if you glance up skywards,
You'll see the strangest sight,
As I join the long migration,
In my 'Micro-Light'.

WHOSE PARTY?

I made a lovely Christmas Cake, for a party treat,
With fruit and nut ingredients, which we love to eat.

Marzipan and icing covered top and edge,
Complete with chubby Santa Claus, on his reindeer sledge.

To prepare a special fare, I toiled the previous day,
Then salads, flans and puddings carefully stored away.

At last the morning dawned for the celebration,
Everyone was seated in happy expectation.

To the kitchen cupboard, I quickly took myself,
But got an awful shock, when I looked upon the shelf.

The door was open wide, and I saw, to my despair,
Our cat had found the windfall, and brought his friends to share.

What a time they'd had, all the food was gone,
And my special Christmas Cake was but a single crumb.

There were no morsels left by the feline troop,
Except some tins of pet food, standing in a group.

The cats were in the garden, tummies blown up fat,
With grins upon their cheeks, just like the 'Cheshire Cat'.

There was nothing left for the family,
So I opened up the 'Pusskins' — and we all had that for tea.

THE GREAT WALL

Our garden wall was crumbling,
It had to be replaced,
A new one then we ordered,
Not knowing what we faced.

Some friendly builders told us,
"We'll make it good as new,
It won't take very long,
Just a week or two."

First they dug foundations,
Twenty metres deep,
Were they for a humble wall,
Or a castle 'keep'?

Cement it came in barrow loads,
By the ton was sand,
Piles of bricks like mountains,
Covered all our land.

The brickworks went on overtime,
To keep the men supplied,
Soon it took a half-hour walk,
To reach the other side.

Finally the copings,
  Were laid along the crest,
A handy skyline perch,
  Where birds now take a rest.

To see the finished rampart,
  Folk came from miles around,
For such a mighty edifice,
  Elsewhere cannot be found.

They say the Wall of China,
  Is the only man-made place,
Which can be seen by Astronauts,
  Far off in outer space.

But another structure surely,
  Will beat this record soon,
They'll see our garden wall as well,
  When next they're on the Moon.

TO BE A COWBOY

I wish I was a Cowboy,
In the great days of the West,
Of all heroic stories,
Their exploits are the best.

With the Sheriff and his Posse,
I'd ride a dusty trail,
To track a gang of outlaws,
And catch them without fail.

Camping on the open plain,
On ground that's hard and dry,
Eating plates of beans,
Beneath a starry sky.

I'd save a town from bandits,
Another battle won,
Then ride a painted pony,
Towards the setting sun.

Alas the 20th Century,
Is right outside my door,
There are no untamed mountains,
The West is wild no more.

Yet still I can pretend,
My home's a ranch house grand,
And stand upon the balcony,
Surveying all my land.

In the midnight darkness,
   When wintry gales blow,
I imagine lowing herds,
   Of woolly Buffalo.

I hear within my dreams,
   Wild Coyotes howl,
But amongst the garden bushes,
   Only Tabbies prowl.

For the ranch is just my Cottage,
   The ranges — but a lawn,
With only friendly Cats,
   To greet the early dawn.

Yet within my home and garden,
   Great things I can achieve,
And bring the past to life,
   In a land of make-believe.

So I don my chaps and stetson,
   Then step outside alone,
To ride my garden prairie,
   And herd the Pussies home.

COOKING THE BOOKS

We're having an annual audit,
   At the office where I work,
Accounts are balanced nicely,
   As no effort do I shirk.

Some papers go in one file,
   And many in another,
Plus those I do not mention,
   Kept quietly undercover.

About these other documents,
   No-one will ever know,
As those correctly entered,
   Are the ones I always show.

Allocating figures,
   Is like dealing packs of cards,
With a little gentle shuffling,
   It isn't very hard.

I realise the Government,
   Is rather short of monev,
But to give them *all* the profit,
   Really isn't funny.

So I'm becoming quite an expert,
   At sorting out the books,
In two sets they're divided,
   For when the Tax-man looks.

And please don't tell a soul,
   Just what I'm really at,
As set 'A' is strictly private,
   Whilst set 'B' is for the VAT!

THE BUILDER'S CLERK

It's a hard life working for a Builder,
Sweat and toil all day,
"Type me this, write out that,"
Anything they say.

Books to add up, answer phone,
Will it ever end?
Glad to get home to relax,
And let myself unwind.

Where they are I never know,
They're wanted here and there,
'Burst pipes, cracked walls and leaking roofs,'
Never an hour to spare.

Problems, problems every day,
For someone to be solving,
It's only willing office staff,
Who keep the wheels turning.

And yet, perhaps it's not so bad,
I still enjoy my task,
To feel one's 'needed' is the best,
So no more could I ask.

Then comes the time, when I retire,
Away from all the strife,
Of bricks and nails and pipes and plugs,
Until that future life —

When up in Heaven, I'll think I'm safe,
And work is far away,
But suddenly, a voice is heard —

"THIS QUOTE MUST GO TODAY!"

WASHING-DAY

Many years ago,
  Before this present time,
Wash-day was a nightmare,
  For trying to shift the grime.

Scrubbing clothes by hand,
  Was all they ever knew,
With an old gas boiler,
  To give the clothes a stew.

Eventually there came,
  A modern day machine,
The clothes were popped inside,
  And came out nice and clean.

So I bought an automatic,
  To help me on my way,
But that washer with a window,
  Eyed me all the day.

Yet with all the new technology,
  This computerized invention,
Was all so complicated,
  And beyond my comprehension.

So many knobs and switches,
  I really didn't know,
Which I should turn or push,
  To make it stop or go.

The other week in haste,
  I pressed the starter button,
Then rushed off to the shops,
  My washing all forgotten.

Returning to the front gate,
  There beneath my feet,
A flood of soapy water,
  Was trickling down the street.

I hurried to the kitchen,
And on opening the door,
A tidal wave of soap suds,
Swept me to the floor.

My metallic monster,
Was gurgling merrily,
It did not even notice,
What was happening to me.

One day my fluffy kitten,
With coat all silky black,
Crept into the drum,
Whilst I had turned my back.

Quite a while later,
How long I do not know,
I opened up the door,
She jumped out — white as snow.

It was then that I decided,
Automation's not for me,
It's surely far less hassle,
To do jobs manually.

There's something to be said,
For the days long past,
At least the work went smoothly,
If not very fast.

So gone are the gadgets,
A good decision made,
And in an Antiques shop,
I found the perfect aid.

It takes a bit of effort,
But the task is rather jolly,
Now I wash by hand,
With a TUB and DOLLY.

KNOTTY PROBLEMS

I joined my Yoga class, a couple of years ago,
Just what I'd let myself in for, I really didn't know.

At first it was quite easy, bend and stretch a little,
And as the weeks went by, I became more supple.

Until one day I realised, beginners' days were over,
When the teacher then requested, I place my leg upon my shoulder.

Arms were folded backwards, twining round each other,
Wrists were crossed, fingers clasped, were they there for ever?

Spinal Twists most certainly suited their names best,
My lower regions faced the East, whilst shoulders were due West.

Struggling to unwind myself, standing up or sitting,
Is rather like attempting to unravel tangled knitting.

Now I'm thinking that, whilst the fun I gain is lots,
I'd make a perfect Sailor, 'cos they've taught me all the knots!

ANOTHER BIRTHDAY

I've had another Birthday,
Which seemed to come so fast,
It really doesn't feel,
Twelve months since the last.

Time goes by more quickly,
With each passing year,
Now my 'pensionable status',
Is drawing very near.

Of the usual accoutrements,
I can take my pick,
Like hearing-aid and spectacles,
Or wooden walking-stick.

When using public transport,
All the passengers will know,
That I've reached the magic sixty,
As a bus pass I must show.

Yet it surely doesn't matter,
What age I am, you see,
Just how young I'm feeling,
Is what means so much to me.

With a little imagination,
Which I never seem to lack,
As time goes marching forwards,
I think, why not also back?

So a decision now I've made,
To go the other way,
And in just a year or two,
I'll be '21 TODAY'.

IF ONLY

I wish I could write poetry,
In a flowing way,
If so I'd make an effort,
To write for you today.

But my words never rhyme,
The phrases are all wrong,
I couldn't put a tune to them,
And turn them into song.

Some lines come out too lengthy,
Others far too short,
I try to search for words,
To make sense of a sort.

My friends are getting tired,
Of calling at my home,
They only hear, when they arrive,
Another ponderous tome.

So I may give up trying,
It doesn't work somehow,
If I only could write poems,
I'd write one for you now.

GHOST TRAIN

A hundred miles from home,
  Late on a winter's day,
I stumbled through the dusk,
  To seek my homeward way.

In the distance, like a sun,
  To greet me, shone a light,
A railway station's friendly glow,
  For me a welcome sight.

Though silent and deserted,
  Was the platform bare,
In the station stood,
  An engine steaming there.

"What is your destination?"
  A young guard then enquired,
I gave him my address,
  He ushered me inside.

Warmth was within the carriage,
  And smooth the journey ran,
Alighting from the train I turned,
  To thank the kindly man.

An older person now was he,
  From just a short while back,
And where the railway line had run,
  Was but a grassy track.

"Where is the train which brought me,
  Safely to my home?
I see no station here now,
  It seems we are alone."

The guard replied in puzzlement,
  "The track sir, don't you know?
This line was closed for ever,
          — 30 Years ago!"

GNOME ARMY

An Auction Sale was taking place,
Just the other day,
In a village hall,
Not so far away.

There was furniture and cutlery,
Rusty cooking pots,
Some crockery was covered,
In funny looking spots.

One item I just fancied,
A handsome garden Gnome,
I thought I'd make a bid,
To give him a good home.

Selling duly started,
The price began to climb,
A final nod from me,
And the Gnome was mine.

Next morning near my door,
A sight then met my eyes,
A regular Gnome army,
Of every shape and size.

Stretching down the street,
In regimented rows,
Then a man commenced,
To carry them indoors.

"What have you brought me here?"
  I mumbled rather dazed,
"Just one Gnome I purchased,"
  The fellow at me gazed.

"When you raised your hand,
  For that one you bid on,
You did not buy just him,
  You bought the whole collection."

Now my house is filled,
  They're standing wall to wall,
And the very tall ones,
  Are packed into the hall.

Gnomes with woolly scarves,
  Some with pointed hats,
And sporty ones with footballs,
  Or clutching cricket bats.

So if you feel your garden,
  Is looking rather bare,
And needs a friendly chappie,
  To fill an odd space there.

Just pop along to my house,
  You can take your pick,
Of any one of hundreds,
  But please . . . .
    Do make it quick!

TO THE SEASIDE

A coach trip out to Blackpool,
Feeling very grand,
We'd go on the amusements,
And stroll along the sands.

Departing early morning,
Arriving before noon,
Only twenty miles or so,
We'd be there very soon.

The countryside flew past us,
And miles slipped quickly by,
We could not recognise the route,
Much as we did try.

Our driver reassured us,
He'd done the trip before,
And soon we'd be deposited,
On the sandy shore.

Passing hills and dales,
Were we getting lost?
This was not the flat terrain,
Along the western coast.

Eight hours after leaving,
  The sea we all espied,
At our destination,
  At last we had arrived.

Then red faced and embarrassed,
  He told us all the truth,
A navigation error,
  Had landed us at BOURNEMOUTH!

So straight back on the coach,
  To start the journey home,
Just that sort of distance,
  We never meant to roam.

But tomorrow we'll be having,
  Our nice day out at last,
With no more fears of getting lost,
  Our worries are all past.

Because: we live at Southport,
  It's all in easy reach,
We'll walk a hundred yards,
  And sit on our own beach.

A WEEK OFF

A week off work on holiday,
What a splendid treat,
I thought I'd take it easy,
And only rest and eat.

A long lie-in each morning,
Breakfast at eleven,
Leisurely strolls around the park,
Was my idea of Heaven.

Lazing in the garden,
Then doze off in the sun,
I'd catch up with my reading,
Life would be such fun.

* * *

But it did not quite turn out,
The way I'd hoped it might,
When the first day I decided,
To put the garden right.

I'd tidy up the undergrowth,
And get the borders weeded,
Just a few hours work,
Was surely all it needed.

The day went swiftly by,
It seemed I'd hardly started,
The weeds refused to budge,
From the ground would not be parted.

That night my back was aching,
Knees all swollen red,
Hands felt like sandpaper,
Could not turn my head.

* * *

Mid-week there was a storm,
The roof then sprang a leak,
So out the ladders came,
To climb the apex peak.

High up on the roof,
Soaking to the skin,
My cotton summer clothes,
Were feeling rather thin.

The hole was duly mended,
And weather changed at last,
But indoors damp wallpaper,
Had to be replaced.

Washing down and scraping,
Then in all my haste,
I slipped on sticky floorboards,
And upset all the paste.

* * *

Next day a letter came,
An invite from a friend,
A day out in the hills,
Was what he did intend.

Just a mile or two,
A pleasant country jaunt,
He'd call round early morning,
At seven a.m. prompt.

Sleepily I joined him,
We set out at a trot,
Twenty miles later,
We staggered to a stop.

Feet all sore with blisters,
  It did not seem to me,
To be as pleasant a hobby,
  As it was meant to be.

Exhaustion and fatigue,
  Had overcome me there,
So there'll be no more holidays,
  Thank goodness, 'til next year.

And I'm happy now because —
  You surely must have guessed,
It's back to work on Monday,
  To have a *proper* rest.

HAPPINESS IS

Happiness is: A pleasant surprise.
Dinner on the table. A smile for everyone.
A warm bed on a cold night.
Remembering someone's Birthday.
Someone remembering your Birthday.
A good deed, asking nothing in return.
Breakfast — and supper — in bed.
Helping someone over the road.
Feeling needed.

Happiness is: No queue at the Post Office.
The TV repair man coming promptly.
The bus — and train — arriving on time.
A tax refund.
Balancing the books.

Happiness is: Hot soup.
Warm socks in winter, bare feet in summer.
Solving the Crossword Puzzle. An interesting book.
Finding the missing article.
Finishing the dusting and hoovering.
Someone else washing-up.
A hot bath and a dry towel.
Comfortable shoes.

Happiness is: Green fields. An English country lane.
The scent of Honeysuckle and Lily of the Valley.
Early morning mist. Dewdrops on petals.
Spring blossom. Summer flowers.
Autumn gold tints. Winter's snowy carpet.
Summer holidays. Swimming in the sea.
A walk in the country.
Your own Garden. Fresh air. A golden Sunset.
Fresh fruit, crisp vegetables.
Birds singing. The 4 a.m. Dawn Chorus.

Happiness is: A letter from home.
Wedding photographs.
Four Cats — or four hundred Cats.
A cuddly Teddy Bear. Coming home.
A good Mother.
A Husband who cares.

OUR LOCAL SHOW

One warm and sunny morning,
  With faces keenly aglow,
We all made our way, to the park for a day,
  At our local Show.

There were colourful fruits and vegetables,
  Which amateur gardeners grow,
The mouth watering sight, filled us all with delight,
  At our local Show.

Displays of pot plants and flowers,
  Were laid out row by row,
The day was so hot, it wilted the lot,
  In our local Show.

A band marched round the arena,
  Playing some tunes we all know,
With the heat over eighty, most players fainted,
  During our local Show.

Four helicopters circled,
  The showground noisy and slow,
The crowd gasped as they, gave a breath-taking display,
  For our local Show.

Ponies and donkeys parading,
  Took fright when they hovered too low,
Then rushed round the park, and were free until dark,
  At our local Show.

Into the tents of produce,
  Did the errant horses go,
They ate all the carrots, prize turnips and parsnips,
  In our local Show.

Some parachutists glided,
  Towards the ground below,
Then floated away, and are lost to this day,
  From our local Show.

Throwing mops at the coconut shy,
  Not very accurately though,
When a man came our way, we knocked off his toupee,
  At our local Show.

Side-shows, lucky dips and bingo,
  On them we all had a go,
And won lots of things, teapots, trinkets and rings,
  During our local Show.

Arms full of gifts we gathered,
  But don't really need them, so,
We're taking them all, to the 'White Elephant' stall,
  At next year's local Show.

COMPUTERIZED

'Life is far more simple,'
The adverts always say,
'With a Home Computer,
So purchase one today.'

'It will do on command,
Anything you please,
Just sit back and enjoy,
A pleasant life of ease.'

But soon the disappointment,
Began to show on me,
It wasn't half as clever,
As I expected it to be.

I hoped it might be useful,
For jobs I don't like much,
Like cooking, cleaning, laundry,
Shopping trips and such.

Yet all it seemed to do,
Was make a funny sound,
Accompanied by some flashing lights,
With digits going round.

The washing-up it never touched,
Pots are there today,
When I offered it the dishcloth,
It looked the other way.

It did not walk the dog,
  Or polish up the shoes,
No meals has it yet prepared,
  The micro' it can't use.

The garden is untouched,
  Roses are not pruned,
For only words and figures,
  My Computer has been tuned.

But I have found at last,
  How it can pay its way,
By teaching me some games,
  I've always longed to play.

Now my housework is neglected,
  I've no clean clothes to wear,
Haven't shopped for weeks,
  The fridge's shelves are bare.

Still what a time I'm having,
  Such fun I can't recall,
Scrabble, Bridge and Chess,
  I'm expert at them all.

CRIMSON POPPIES

Many years ago,
   Down a country lane
A field of crimson poppies,
   Set the earth aflame.

But time it soon caught up,
   With that unspoilt land,
Along came urban people,
   Their business to expand.

Away went all the wild flowers,
   Trees and little creatures,
Replaced by large brick buildings,
   With grey and daunting features.

Grassy tracks of dust,
   Were widened into roads,
Enabling heavy transport,
   To carry larger loads.

Soon the mills were opened,
   Folks flocked in to work,
Machinery clattered,
   From morning until dark.

Yet times of change arrived,
   After years nigh on a hundred,
The business was declining,
   Its days of glory numbered.

Away went the employees,
  Management and all,
The buildings were demolished,
  Each chimney, roof and wall.

Once more the land was hushed,
  Few sounds could be heard,
Just some buzzing bees,
  And the singing of a bird.

Barren, bleak and empty,
  The site was left alone,
For Nature to take over,
  And claim what was her own.

Slowly over decades,
  Helped by sun and rain,
Little shoots appeared,
  To see the world again.

Across the ancient meadow,
  A flame of red now burned,
The wheel had come full circle,
  — And poppies had returned.

SEEING THE WORLD

I travel round the World,
   Each year many times,
From hot and sandy deserts,
   To chilly Arctic climes.

Across the wildest Continents,
   Fearsome lions roar,
Curious creatures greet me,
   As the jungles I explore.

Trips to Northern Regions,
   Where Polar Bears do roam,
Or the ice lands of Antarctica,
   To see the Penguins' home.

I dive in deepest oceans,
   Where the sea is clear and calm,
Parachute from blue skies,
   With not a single qualm.

The mysteries of the Orient,
   Are opened up for me,
Sacred Tombs and Palaces,
   All are there to see.

Discovering Ancient Monuments,
  Castles, Forts and Temples,
Built in times long past,
  By Greek and Roman peoples.

I explore Earth's greatest caverns,
  Into the depth and gloom,
And watch intrepid spacemen,
  Start their journeys to the Moon.

A wealth of different sports,
  Taking place in many lands,
Olympic Games and Championships,
  I see them at close hand.

Aboard the mighty Concorde,
  Faster than the speed of sound,
Or the graceful Q.E.2,
  As she is ocean bound.

These delights are mine to savour,
  As a crystal ball to wish on,
I visit them in comfort,
  Via *Colour Television*.

CYCLING IS FUN

I used to go out cycling,
  Keenly every day,
To keep me fit and healthy,
  I pedalled on my way.

Heat waves in the summer,
  Left me hot and bothered,
Still I was undaunted,
  As the countryside I covered.

Rain and sleet were tackled,
  East winds which did wail,
With head tucked down against them,
  I pushed on through the hail.

Freezing in the winter,
  Skin as cold as steel,
Fingers numb and aching,
  And toes I could not feel.

But the novelty of having,
  Frost-bite or sunburn,
Was wearing rather thin,
  For comforts I did yearn.

It seemed the local scenery,
Underwent some changes,
What were once grassy fields,
Were now like mountain ranges.

Each hill felt, as I puffed up,
Five miles to the crown,
Yet mysteriously was only,
One mile coming down.

But now I've solved the problem,
And I'm feeling very pleased,
No more aching muscles,
Or painful swollen knees.

Those days are long since over,
My struggling is done,
I bicycle still daily,
In a way that's much more fun.

It may rain or gales may blow,
Yet I'll cycle when I like,
Now I have the last laugh,
On my *Indoor Exercise Bike!*

LIVING NEAR THE AIRPORT

Five miles down the road, a runway stretches out,
'International Airport' the signposts loudly shout.

Each minute one plane leaves they say, for many a distant shore,
But it sounds like every second, listening to the roar.

A million passengers a month, the Airlines proudly cheer,
Yet what of deafened residents, suffering down here.

Can't view television, as we cannot hear the sound,
So we sit and watch the fish tank, with the Guppies swimming round.

Nights with windows tightly closed, but still we wake from slumber,
As the bed shakes like as Aspen, to a roar like thunder.

It's only one more '747' gliding over roof-tops,
Barely missing aerials, as it neatly skims the chimney-pots.

Mention tea out in the garden, and we are not amused,
Folding seats and deck-chairs, are stored away unused.

Conversation's limited, we both know how to mime,
And rush in for the ear-plugs, yet another time.

So one day we'll pack our bags, and take an Airport bus,
To buy a one-way ticket, for our reluctant exodus.

We won't miss the massive Jumbos, and the friendly slimline Concordes,
As we listen to the silence, or the singing of the birds.

In the middle of an ocean, a little Island lies,
So if you see two parachutes, descending from the skies.

You'll know we're leaving England, for ever and a day,
To spend our lives in peace and quiet —
FAR, FAR AWAY!

FOUR CATS AND A HUSBAND

Four cats and a husband,
What a lot of work,
To keep them fit and happy,
Nothing will I shirk.

Shopping in the precinct,
Food for dinner and tea,
I'm sure the local stores,
Make a fortune out of me.

Hoovering the carpets,
Dusting in the hall,
It seems my life is mainly,
At their beck and call.

For them it's one long holiday,
Without a single care,
Whether ambling round the garden,
Or settling in a chair.

Here's the supper ready,
Their favourite one again,
With such a wholesome appetite,
Nothing will remain.

Comfy beds to sleep in,
Clean blankets fresh as new,
Keeps them all contented,
So what more can I do?

But in spite of all the effort,
I still have time to smile,
Four cats and a husband,
Make my life worthwhile.

EASTER

The other morning, quite by chance,
I called at Heaven's gate,
Doors were shut and well secured,
Signs said 'Kindly Wait'.

A voice enquired "Who is it there?"
I meekly then replied,
"No-one important, only me,
Is there room inside?"

"No-one important; that can't be,"
I heard the gateman say,
"We all are needed in this life,
And have our part to play.

"You cannot leave this Earth right now,
There's far too much to do,
Who is going to carry on,
The work that's left by you?

"You must know, that, at Easter time,
All the World's reborn,
Baby birds and animals,
Appearing every morn.

"The buds are bursting into flower,
New leaves adorn the trees,
The scent of blossom carries far,
Upon the gentle breeze.

"Who will teach the baby birds,
  The newest songs to sing,
And help them find their way about,
  When they take to the wing?

"Someone has to give a help,
  To little creatures here,
As they begin their struggle,
  Into a life so dear.

"And, as the years go quickly by,
  They'll grow adult and grand,
With their own little ones who'll need,
  A willing, helpful hand.

"The years stretch out for you to spread,
  Your love far and away,
Inspired by one who lives again,
  This happy Easter Day.

"So, when these tasks are all complete,
  Don't rush away and hide,
But come once more, and you will find,
  The gates are open wide."

CHRISTMAS

I travelled several days and nights,
  To where I did not know,
Yet in the distance there, could see,
  A constant starry glow.

Many lands I seemed to cross,
  Within a single day,
All the peoples of the World,
  Gathered on my way.

Finally my home I reached,
  Late on a Christmas Eve,
How I had traversed all those miles,
  I scarcely could believe.

A sound I heard that evening late,
  Outside where snow was deep,
There was a lowly neighing,
  Which lulled me into sleep.

A crystal winter's morning,
  Awoke me from the night,
I peered into the stable yard,
  To see the strangest sight.

Donkey's hoof marks in the snow,
Besides the prints of man,
From an empty stable shone,
A warm glow there within.

Among the stalls were gathered,
God's creatures large and small,
They gazed in awe and wonder,
Their bright eyes told me all.

Not just for me this mystery,
But everyone in need,
Of saving from all wrongful ways,
A better life to lead.

Through their eyes, the souls shone out,
And nowhere else on Earth,
Could I look in, and see right there,
The meaning of a birth.

ENGLAND IN THE SUMMER

How beautiful is England,
On a summer's day,
The cheerful sun and blue sky,
Sweep our cares away.

Out comes garden furniture,
Deck-chairs slightly torn,
Plastic cups and saucers,
High teas upon the lawn.

Dishes filled with salads,
Ice-cool fruity drinks,
Reclining couch and sunshade,
For snatching forty winks.

Bees are softly humming,
As they buzz from flower to flower,
We lie and watch them lazily,
Enjoying every hour.

Tennis on the grass courts,
Cricket in the park,
Swimming at the lido,
From morning until dark.

But what is in the distance?
   Can it be, oh no;
Clouds loom ominously,
   A breeze begins to blow.

First a pitter-patter,
   Then it starts to pour,
Suddenly a cloudburst,
   And we all rush for the door.

Yet we English are stalwart,
   And take what comes our way,
Be it heat waves in mid-winter,
   Or a chilly August day.

So come on, altogether now,
   And sing this bright refrain,
"Nowhere could be nicer,
   Than England in the rain."

TED

Who is the best pal we could need,
Why Ted of course, a friend indeed.

Always honest, always true,
He shares his life with me and you.

If we are lonely, there is no fear,
Faithful Ted is ever near.

Someone to talk to quietly,
For hours he listens patiently.

Happiness is two bright eyes,
Woolly paws, and face so wise.

Giving joy without measure,
Teddy is our greatest treasure.

Soft and cuddly, fur all curled,
Everybody in the World,

Loves a Teddy Bear.

THE LAST CHIMNEY

Nigh on a hundred years it stood,
A landmark in the town,
But then one day they blew it up,
And History tumbled down.

A stately chimney, tall and slim,
Through times of peace and war,
No storm or tempest damaged it,
But now it stands no more.

Human hands and dynamite,
A lethal combination,
One moment, proudly standing there,
In seconds — devastation.

The bricks are moved, the site is cleared,
Construction work begins,
Yet in the early morning mist,
A shadow still remains.

We cannot wipe out yesterday,
In just a single hour,
Be it houses, mills or factories,
A chimney or a tower.

Buildings come and buildings go,
And life goes quietly on,
But as it vanished in the dust,
It seemed a friend had gone.

As years pass by, our memory stays,
And ghostly forms appear,
Thus evermore we still shall see,
The chimney standing here.

MAGIC OF THE MOVIES

Bring back the days of Cinema,
The magic movie show,
Nostalgia for the old times,
Still sets our hearts aglow.

Saturday morning rendezvous,
What fun for youngsters there,
We saw our hero Superman,
And exploits of Dan Dare.

Alive came ancient Romans,
The Empire of the Caesars,
Better than the history books,
Could ever hope to teach us.

We rode the range on horses,
With Roy Rogers and Tom Mix,
Fought the battle of the Alamo,
And all for one-and-six.

From humble corner picture house,
To towering 'Majestic',
They'd show an old 'B' Western,
With the latest 3-hour Epic.

Whether plush seats in the Balcony,
And carpets wall to wall,
Or wooden floor and benches,
We frequented them all.

The crowded Auditorium,
  Was hushed as Jolson sang,
And with his songs of Dixie,
  Echoes of the Deep South rang.

In the Universe of darkness,
  A journey to the stars,
Leaving Earth behind us,
  For Jupiter or Mars.

But sadly now those days are gone,
  Together with our dreams,
And Bingo fills the stages,
  Where stood the silver screens.

We watch TV in our houses,
  But this is not the same,
As the thrill of queuing hours,
  To see our heroes once again.

Well, let us keep on hoping,
  The day is not too far,
When they convert each Supermarket,
  Back into a Cinema.

PAINTING THE HOUSE

The sun is shining, Summer's here,
Going to paint the house this year.

Paint is purchased, and a brush,
Get out the ladders, what a rush.

Scraping, brushing, rubbing down,
White, blue, orange, pink and brown.

Five layers thick upon each other,
Have to come off, what a bother.

Blowlamp working overtime,
Ready for the sand and prime.

A friendly dog, who makes a fuss,
Upsets a brand-new tin of gloss.

Our smart front door is carefully painted,
Then pussy comes and rubs against it.

Windy days and all forlorn,
Why did I have to mow the lawn?

Grass and trimmings from the hedges,
Have stuck to doors and window-ledges.

I start to do it all again,
But alas, it pours with rain.

Thunder, hail and lightning streaks,
Keep me housebound two full weeks.

Then happiness, it's fine once more,
Must start again my mammoth chore.

This house is average, so I thought,
But it feels like tackling 'Hampton Court'.

Arms are aching, shoulders seized,
Cannot bend my swollen knees.

Never mind, I must not slacken,
It's worth the effort being taken.

Finally the work is done,
Stand back, admire my marathon.

Is my wife pleased? Well no, you see,
A slight mistake was made by me.

I got it wrong, the colour scheme,
1 It's red and yellow — she wanted GREEN.

GOING ABROAD

I've just returned from holiday,
  "Algarve, this year" I said,
Never been abroad before,
  And heard it beats the 'Med',
The flying rather worried me,
  It's something which I dread.

At the Airport I arrived,
  Many hours too soon,
With a million other folk,
  One rainy afternoon,
When we packed onto the plane,
  To breathe there wasn't room.

Down the runway, off we went,
  Just like racing cars,
Climbing up eternally,
  Passing several stars,
I wondered if my holiday,
  Was Portugal — or Mars!

For hours we soared across the sky,
  Fearing we were stranded,
To spend my life above the clouds,
  It seemed fate had me branded,
At last, the tarmac came in view,
  And finally we landed.

The holiday was lots of fun,
  Warm sand and deep blue sea,
The sun was very, very hot,
  Frying all of me,
Two weeks later and I was,
  As tired as could be.

Coming back and down to earth,
  Is not so bad you know,
My home's my castle, even when,
  The gales begin to blow,
But come next year in summer-time,
  It's off again I'll go.

So back to work tomorrow,
  But wearing — dare I say?
Natty shorts and 'T' shirt,
  They're all I have today,
Since the Airline left my luggage,
  Somewhere far away.

FAREWELL, MY HORSE

'Twas long ago when last I rode,
Through fields and country wide,
With you a gallant friend, my horse,
A handsome steed, my pride.

The summer days were long and warm,
What fun we had together,
Canters down the sandy beach,
And trotting through the heather.

We galloped through the meadows,
Where buttercups abound,
And paused by wayside verges,
To hear the crickets' sound.

But time it passes for us all,
You had to leave this world and me,
And as I walk our trails alone,
One day, united, I know we'll be.

I long to see again your eyes,
Of kindly chocolate brown,
The gentle muzzle, soft as silk,
And coat as smooth as down.

Your stable now is dark and empty,
  The manger, bare of oats and hay,
Around the field, silent shadows,
  Yet still I hear a quiet neigh.

I can no longer stroke your mane,
  Or brush the bracken from your tail,
So here I sit and write of you,
  Memories which never fail.

Among the clover covered pastures,
  The grass is greener now for you,
A Paradise for horses,
  Eternal sun, with skies of blue.

Across the fields of Heaven,
  I'll call to you again,
And gone will be the years of waiting,
  When God shall rein me in.

ROAD WORKS

They dug the road up round our way,
A little hole at first,
"It's just a tiny job" they said,
"A simple water burst."

The gap grew bigger every day,
The mound of earth enlarged,
It covered kerb and footpath,
Engulfing several cars.

The men went deeper, down and down,
Right through seams of coal,
We could not see them any more,
But heard they had struck oil.

Heaps of sand and soil increased,
Resembling Alpine mountains,
The summits vanished into cloud,
And surely reached the Heavens.

Our water turned a funny colour,
Muddy brown and hazy,
Should we drink it? Better not,
In case it makes us queasy.

A few days later, from the hole,
The men appeared at last,
Jubilant and full of smiles,
"Now we've repaired that burst."

No sooner had they packed and gone,
Taking all their tools,
When 'British Gas' arrived outside,
To dig some larger holes.

New gas mains were finally down,
  Oh goodness; what a blessing,
Holes were filled, paths were swept,
  The end of all our suffering.

But then today, quite near our door,
  There they were — more vans,
Dumper trucks, pneumatic drills,
  Traffic-lights and cones.

"Electric Board" they all announced,
  "We have to lay new cable,
You won't mind just a little noise,
  We'll finish when we're able."

"What no power?" we then exclaimed,
  "And in this freezing weather,"
But hardy residents don't *need*,
  Electric, gas and water.

Friends won't call round any more,
  They cannot reach our home,
They seem to think we're living in,
  A demolition zone.

And guess what's coming next, because,
  The telephone is dead,
Now Telecom inform us that,
  New phone lines must be laid.

We cannot beat them, so we'll join them,
  Here's bucket and spade from me,
Let's play in all the sand-hills,
  And pretend we're by the sea!

HOPE

This World of ours is moving,
In an automatic age,
Speed boats, hi-fis, motor cars,
Computers and jet planes.

But we can't go on forever,
Building larger, faster, stronger,
When we lay the final concrete,
We may see the earth no longer.

When falls the last small petal,
From the final flower which grew,
And there are no more gardens,
Nor country, or sea-view.

Then shall we see the folly,
Of our artificial ways?
And long to turn full circle,
To those slower, peaceful days.

We must not ignore Nature,
With the benefits she gives,
Fresh air, good health and beauty,
In living, natural things.

But we need never worry,
At this fast and frenzied pace,
For the day will soon be dawning,
On a calmer, quiet age.

The rattle of machinery,
  One day will fade away,
Horse and carriage will return,
  To town and country lane.

The traffic jam of ages,
  Will choke cars from off the roads,
Trees will grow where tarmac,
  Spans the land from coast to coast.

From way back through the ages,
  Hear the sound in all the land,
As the coachman calls out gently,
  To his eager four-in-hand.

If you listen very carefully,
  Can you hear the echo now?
The neighing and the snorting,
  Of Clydesdales to the plough.

Again we'll find a pleasure,
  In a daily walk to see,
Wild plants by the wayside,
  The hedgerows and the trees.

For the happy day *will* come,
  When the sun shines not in vain,
On flowers, birds and animals,
  And the World will smile again.

MY FOUR CATS

Fast asleep,
  My four Cats,
In their world of dreams.

Yawning, stretching,
  Waking up,
Time for purrs and preens.

Now it's playtime,
  Round and round,
Catch me if you will.

Through the garden,
  And the house,
Every chair's a hill.

Is it tea-time?
  Jolly good,
We are hungry too.

One dish each,
  Who eats most,
Is it me or you?

Washing whiskers,
  Cleaning spats,
And —
Fast asleep,
  My four Cats.